Can You Tell the Difference?

Is it a Bee or a Wasp?

Gail Terp

BLACK
RABBIT
BOOKS

Hi Jinx is published by Black Rabbit Books
P.O. Box 3263, Mankato, Minnesota, 56002.
www.blackrabbitbooks.com
Copyright © 2020 Black Rabbit Books

Marysa Storm, editor; Michael Sellner, designer;
Omay Ayres, photo researcher

Library of Congress
Cataloging-in-Publication Data
Names: Terp, Gail, 1951- author.
Title: Is it a bee or a wasp? / by Gail Terp.
Description: Mankato, Minnesota : Black Rabbit Books, [2020] |
Series: Hi jinx. Can you tell the difference? | Audience:
Age 9-12. | Audience: Grade 4 to 6. | Includes
bibliographical references and index.
Identifiers: LCCN 2018024285 (print) | LCCN 2018025493
(ebook) | ISBN 9781680729030
(e-book) | ISBN 9781680728972
(library binding) | ISBN
9781644660522 (paperback)
Subjects: LCSH: Bees–Juvenile
literature. | Wasps–Juvenile
literature.
Classification: LCC QL565.2 (ebook) |
LCC QL565.2 .T47 2020 (print) |
DDC 595.79/9-dc23
LC record available at
https://lccn.loc.gov/2018024285

Printed in China. 1/19

Image Credits

Contents

CHAPTER 1

What Is It?. 5

CHAPTER 2

All about Bees
and Wasps. 9

CHAPTER 3

Tell the Difference. . . .18

CHAPTER 4

Get in on the Hi Jinx. .20

Other Resources. 22

4

Chapter 1
What Is It?

You are on a hike in the woods. You're surrounded by tall trees with bright green leaves. All around you, insects are at work. You grab a peach from your backpack and take a juicy bite. Soon, a bee lands on your peach. Wait. It could be a wasp. You swat the shiny insect away. Uh-oh! The bug is no longer interested in your peach. It's flying straight at you. You'd better drop the peach and run!

A Lot in Common

Bees and wasps have a lot in common. They're both winged insects that often have yellow stripes. Bees and wasps live all around the world. And they both dislike being swatted. (Who doesn't?)

At first, it can be hard to tell them apart. But bees and wasps do have their differences. Read on to learn about them.

There are about 20,000 known **species** of bees.

There are about 30,000 known species of wasps.

bee

wasp

8

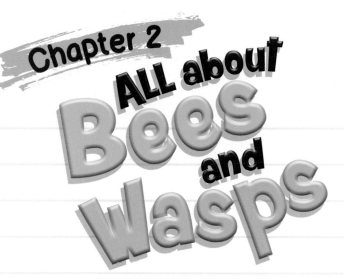

Chapter 2
ALL about Bees and Wasps

Bees and wasps have many different **traits**. For example, their bodies are different. Bees have round, hairy bodies. They use their hair to collect **pollen** from flowers. Wasp bodies are slim and smooth. Their bodies aren't nearly as hairy. They're usually a bit shiny too.

Bees carry pollen from flower to flower. This pollination helps the plants make seeds.

Look at the Legs

If you happen to get close to a bee or wasp, check out the legs. (Don't get too close, though. They like their personal space!) Bee legs are hairy, like their bodies. Their leg hair also collects and carries pollen. Wasp legs are long, thin, and mostly hairless.

On the Attack

Wasps are more **aggressive** than bees. An angry wasp is much more likely to chase you down. Then things can get terribly unpleasant. A wasp can sting you over and over.

A honeybee can only sting you once. After stinging, it dies. Other types of bees can sting more than once. But they aren't likely to.

Do not get stung by a bee or wasp to figure out what it is!

Finding Food

These insects also eat different things. Bees are usually the ones you see buzzing around flowers. They like the pollen and **nectar**. Wasps, on the other hand, feast on juicy insects. They like sweet drinks and fruit too.

Wasps eat many kinds of insects. Some even lay their eggs in insects. The eggs hatch, and the **larvae** eat the insects' guts.

beehive

beehive box

wasp nest

16

Paper or Wax?

Bees and wasps also make different kinds of homes. Bees build their nests using wax that they make. They build in trees or underground holes. If beekeepers put out beehive boxes, they'll use them too.

Wasp nests are made of paper, not wax. They look a bit like ugly piñatas. Don't even think about whacking them, though!

Wasps make paper by chewing wood fiber into **pulp**.

Chapter 3

Tell the Difference

Bees and wasps might look a lot alike. But they actually have many differences.

- eat pollen and nectar
- less aggressive
- more aggressive
- eat insects and fruit
- wax nests
- paper nests
- round bodies
- slim bodies
- hairy bodies and legs
- mostly hairless bodies and legs

A

B

Is It a
Bee
or a
Wasp?

C

D

Chapter 4
Get in on the Hi Jinx

Humans aren't the only creatures that like to dance. A honeybee is always on the lookout for pollen or nectar. When a honeybee finds a food source, it goes to its hive. At the hive, it dances. This dance shows the other honeybees where to find the food.

Take It One Step More

1. Wasps are more aggressive than bees. Why do you think that is?

2. Why is wax better than paper for beehives? Do some research to find out.

3. Make a **Venn diagram** using bee and wasp features. Do you think they are more alike or different?

A. bee   B. wasp   C. bee   D. wasp

GLOSSARY

aggressive (uh-GRES-iv)—showing a readiness to fight, argue, or attack

fiber (FI-burh)—mostly indigestible material in food

larva (LAR-vuh)—the wormlike form of an animal after hatching from an egg

nectar (NEK-tuhr)—a sweet liquid given off by planets and flowers

pollen (PAHL-en)—powdery, yellow grains on flowering plants

pulp (PUHLP)—a material prepared usually from wood or rags and used in making paper

species (SPEE-seez)—a class of individuals that have common characteristics and share a common name

trait (TREYT)—a characteristic or quality

Venn diagram (VEN DAHY-uh-gram)— a diagram that shows the relationship between two groups of things by means of overlapping circles

BOOKS

Esbaum, Jill. *Honey Bees.* Explore My World. Washington, D.C.: National Geographic Kids, 2017.

Gish, Ashley. *Wasps.* Insects. Mankato, MN: Creative Education, 2018.

Pearson, Scott. *Africanized Honeybees.* Invasive Species Takeover. North Mankato, MN: Black Rabbit Books, 2017.

WEBSITES

Bee or Wasp?
www.cbc.ca/kidscbc2/the-feed/bee-or-wasp

Bees and Wasps
www.dkfindout.com/us/animals-and-nature/insects/bees-and-wasps/

Honeybee
kids.nationalgeographic.com/animals/honeybee/#honeybee-pink-flower.jpg

INDEX

F

food, 9, 14, 15, 18

H

hair, 9, 10, 18

L

legs, 10, 18

N

nests, 17, 18

R

ranges, 6

S

stings, 13

W

wings, 6